THE ROSARY

BY
FR MICHAEL SHARKEY

alive Publishing

First published in 2018 by Alive Publishing Ltd
Graphic House, 124 City Road, Stoke on Trent, ST4 2PH
Tel: +44 (0) 1782 745600 • Fax: +44 (0) 1782 745500
www.alivepublishing.co.uk • email: booksales@alivepublishing.co.uk

© 2018 Alive Publishing. British Library Catalogue-in-Publication Data.
A catalogue record for this book is available from the British Library.

Scripture texts used in this publication are taken from the Jerusalem
Bible and the Revised Standard Version Bible.

In the United Kingdom such licences are issued by the Publishers
Licencing Society Ltd, 90 Tottenham Court Road, London W1P 9HE.

Imprimatur: Archbishop Bernard Longley, 2018. Nihil Obstat: Fr
Paul Dean MA, STB, MA. The nihil obstat and imprimatur are official
declarations that a book or pamphlet is free from doctrinal or moral
error. No implication is contained therein that those who have granted
the nihil obstat or imprimatur agree with the content, opinions or
statements expressed.

ISBN: 978-1-906278-27-4

INTRODUCTION

A Rosary is a "garland of roses" i.e. prayers. Popular tradition attributes the Rosary to Saint Dominic, the founder of the Order of Preachers (Dominicans) in 1214. Repetitive prayer was introduced to the Church in the 3rd and 4th centuries. Knots were put into cords to keep count of the number of times a prayer had been said, usually 50 or 150. The Jesus Prayer was the most popular. (Lord Jesus Christ, Son of the living God, have mercy on me, a sinner.) The Dominicans divided the 50 knots into five bunches of ten "Hail Marys" (decades), added an "Our Father" at the beginning and a "Glory be" at the end. Then, they attributed to each decade a particular "mystery", meaning an event or episode in the life of Jesus and his mother Mary. So, there are five Joyful Mysteries, five Sorrowful Mysteries, and five Glorious Mysteries. In 2002 Pope John Paul II added five Luminous Mysteries.

HOW TO USE YOUR ROSARY BEADS

Some people use their fingers to keep track of their rosary prayers. Others use a simple rosary ring. Most people, though, use a set of beads.

The Rosary begins with the sign of the cross (holding the crucifix, if using a set of beads):

In the name of the Father, and of the Son, and of the Holy Spirit.

Then (still holding the crucifix) the Apostles' Creed:

I believe in God, the Father almighty,
Creator of heaven and earth,
and in Jesus Christ, his only Son, our Lord,
who was conceived by the Holy Spirit,
born of the Virgin Mary,
suffered under Pontius Pilate,
was crucified, died and was buried;
he descended into hell;

on the third day he rose again from the dead;
he ascended into heaven,
and is seated at the right hand of God the Father almighty;
from there he will come to judge the living and the dead.
I believe in the Holy Spirit, the holy catholic Church, the
communion of saints the forgiveness of sins, the resurrection
of the body, and life everlasting. Amen.

GLORY BE

HAIL MARY

OUR FATHER

There are five beads connecting the crucifix
to the main rosary.

On the first you say the Our Father,
On the next three you say Hail Marys,
And on the fifth you say the Glory be.

1 Then, you begin each mystery with
   the Our Father
2 Continue through ten Hail Marys
3 And end with the Glory be.

Using the same bead with which you
concluded the last mystery, you begin
the next with the Our Father; and so on
through the five mysteries.

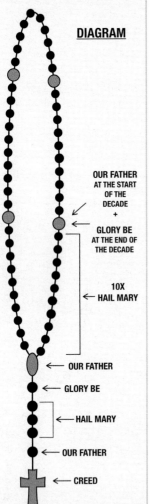

DIAGRAM

OUR FATHER
AT THE START
OF THE
DECADE
+
GLORY BE
AT THE END
OF THE DECADE

10X
← HAIL MARY

← OUR FATHER

← GLORY BE

← HAIL MARY

← OUR FATHER

← CREED

There are three ways of praying the Rosary. You can think about the words as you say them. You can think about the mystery, even entering into it in imagination. Or you can think about the intention that you are praying about. Or you can let your mind move through all three.

All prayer is addressed to God, but what is so delightful with the Rosary is that we can pray in Our Lady's company and with her support.

It is recommended that:
The Joyful Mysteries
are prayed on -
Monday and Saturday
The Sorrowful Mysteries -
Tuesday and Friday
The Glorious Mysteries -
Wednesday and Sunday
The Luminous Mysteries -
Thursday

THE ROSARY PRAYERS

In the name of the Father and of the Son and of the Holy Spirit. Amen.

Our Father, who art in heaven,
hallowed be thy name.
Thy kingdom come.
Thy will be done on earth as it is in heaven.
Give us this day our daily bread,
and forgive us our trespasses
as we forgive those who trespass against us.
And lead us not into temptation,
but deliver us from evil. Amen.

Hail Mary, full of grace, the Lord is with thee; blessed art thou among women, and blessed is the fruit of thy womb, Jesus. Holy Mary, Mother of God, pray for us sinners, now, and at the hour of our death. Amen.

Glory be to the Father and to the Son and to the Holy Spirit, as it was in the beginning, is now and ever shall be, world without end. Amen.

At the end of the Rosary:

Hail, holy Queen, Mother of mercy; hail, our life, our sweetness and our hope. To thee do we cry, poor banished children of Eve, to thee do we send up our sighs, mourning and weeping in this vale of tears. Turn, then, most gracious Advocate, thine eyes of mercy towards us, and after this, our exile, show unto us the blessed fruit of thy womb, Jesus. O clement, O loving, O sweet Virgin Mary.
Pray for us, O holy Mother of God,
That we may be made worthy of the promises of Christ.

Pour forth, we beseech you, O Lord, your grace into our hearts, that we to whom the Incarnation of Christ your Son was made known by the message of an Angel, may be brought to the glory of his Resurrection. Who lives and reigns for ever and ever. Amen.

In the name of the Father and of the Son and of the Holy Spirit. Amen.

THE JOYFUL MYSTERIES

THE ANNUNCIATION

The angel Gabriel was sent by God to a town in Galilee called Nazareth, to a virgin engaged to a man named Joseph. The virgin's name was Mary. The angel said to her, "Hail, Mary, full of grace, the Lord is with you. Do not be afraid, Mary, for you have found favour with God. He wants you to conceive and give birth to a son, and you must call him Jesus." "How can this be," said Mary, "since I am a virgin?" The power of the Most High will come upon you," said the angel, "so the child will be holy, the Son of God." "I am the handmaid of the Lord," said Mary. "Let what you have said be done to me."

OUR FATHER..., TEN HAIL MARYS..., GLORY BE...

THE VISITATION

Elizabeth was barren and was getting on in years. The angel Gabriel had appeared to her husband Zechariah and predicted that Elizabeth would give birth to a son, and they must name him John. Elizabeth was six months pregnant when Mary visited her. When Elizabeth heard Mary's greeting, the child in her womb leapt for joy, and she cried out to Mary, "Blessed are you among women, and blessed is the fruit of your womb". And Mary said, "My soul magnifies the Lord and my spirit rejoices in God my Saviour." Mary stayed with Elizabeth about three months, and then went back home to Nazareth.

OUR FATHER..., TEN HAIL MARYS..., GLORY BE...

THE NATIVITY

Caesar Augustus ordered that a census of the whole world be made. So Mary and Joseph travelled to Bethlehem, the city of David, because Joseph was of David's house and line. The time came for Mary to have her child, but there was no room for them in the inn, so Mary gave birth in a stable and laid her child in a manger. An angel appeared to shepherds who were guarding their sheep and told them of the birth, so the shepherds made haste and found Mary and Joseph and the child lying in a manger. Some wise men from the east followed a star until it led them to where the child lay. They went inside and found the child with his mother Mary. They fell on their knees and offered him gifts of gold, frankincense and myrrh.

OUR FATHER..., TEN HAIL MARYS..., GLORY BE...

THE PRESENTATION

Mary and Joseph took the child Jesus up to Jerusalem to present him in the temple, as laid down in the law of Moses. Simeon was there, a just and upright man, to whom it had been revealed by the Holy Spirit that he would not see death until he had seen the Christ. He took the child in his arms and said, "At last, all-powerful Master, you give leave to your servant to go in peace, according to your promise. For my eyes have seen your salvation which you have prepared for all nations, the light to enlighten the Gentiles and give glory to Israel, your people." Then, turning to Mary, he added, "A sword of sorrow will pierce your own soul too." When Mary and Joseph had done all that the law of the Lord required, they went back home to Nazareth; and the child grew.

OUR FATHER..., TEN HAIL MARYS..., GLORY BE...

THE FINDING IN THE TEMPLE

Every year the Holy Family went up to Jerusalem to celebrate the Feast of Passover. When Jesus was twelve years old, they went up as usual. When the feast was over, Mary and Joseph set off home. They presumed that Jesus was travelling with the caravan, but when they looked for him they could not find him. So they returned to Jerusalem to search for him and found him on the third day. He was in the temple, listening to the teachers and asking them questions. And all who heard him were amazed at his wisdom and insight. His mother said to him, "How could you do this to us? We have been so worried." Jesus answered, "Did you not know that I must be about my Father's business?" But he went down with them to Nazareth and was obedient to them; and Mary remembered all these things in her heart.

OUR FATHER..., TEN HAIL MARYS..., GLORY BE...

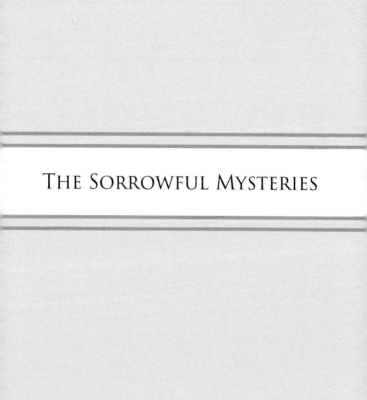

THE SORROWFUL MYSTERIES

THE AGONY IN THE GARDEN

Jesus celebrated his Last Supper with the Apostles on the Feast of Passover. Afterwards he took them to the Garden of Gethsemane. He took Peter, James and John further into the garden, saying "My soul is sorrowful, even unto death". His mental agony had begun. Going forward alone, he fell on his knees and prayed, "Father, if it be possible, let this chalice pass from me. Nevertheless, let your will be done, not mine." His sweat became like great drops of blood falling to the ground. He returned three times to the three apostles and found them asleep. "Could you not watch one hour with me ? The spirit is willing, but the flesh is weak. Now the hour has come when the Son of Man is betrayed into the hands of sinners." And Judas came up and kissed him.

OUR FATHER..., TEN HAIL MARYS..., GLORY BE...

THE SCOURGING AT THE PILLAR

Jesus was taken for trial, first before the Sanhedrin, the Jewish court, where he was accused of blasphemy for claiming to be the Son of God, and where Caiaphas, the High Priest had said "It is better for one man to die for the sake of the people, rather than the whole nation be destroyed"; then, before Pilate, the Roman authority, accused of opposing taxes to Caesar. Pilate said, "I find no case against him;" but learning that Jesus was from Galilee, he sent him to Herod who had jurisdiction there. Herod was keen to witness a miracle, but Jesus was silent, so Herod sent him back to Pilate, who said, "This man has done nothing wrong that deserves death, so I shall have him flogged and then let him go." But the crowd cried "Crucify him ! Crucify him!" Pilate said , "You have a custom that I release a prisoner for you at the time of the Passover. I propose to release Jesus." But the crowd cried, "Give us Barabbas!" So Pilate ordered the death of Jesus and sent him to be scourged. The blood-letting had begun.

OUR FATHER..., TEN HAIL MARYS..., GLORY BE...

The Crowning with Thorns

"So, you are a king?" asked Pilate. Jesus replied, "My kingdom is not of this world." The soldiers took Jesus, stripped him, and put a purple robe on him. Then they plaited a crown of thorns and put it on his head, and they put a reed in his right hand. Then they mocked him. "Hail, King of the Jews!" They spat on him, and took the reed and hit him on the head with it. Jesus, wearing the crown of thorns and the purple robe, was brought out before the crowd. "Behold, the man," said Pilate. "Crucify him, crucify him!" the crowd shouted again. "Shall I crucify your king?" said Pilate. "We have no king but Caesar," answered the chief priests. Then the soldiers took away the purple robe, put Jesus's own clothes back on him, and led him away to be crucified.

Our Father..., Ten Hail Marys..., Glory be...

THE CARRYING OF THE CROSS

Now the sins of the world are laid on your shoulder to be carried by you to Calvary and to death. So heavy is your burden that you falter and you fall, and you fall and fall again. On you lies a punishment which brings us peace, for you are the Suffering Servant of all mankind, without beauty, without majesty, no looks to attract our eyes, a thing despised and rejected by men, a man of sorrows familiar with suffering, draining away in the gutter. You met your mother, consoled the women of Jerusalem, and received the help of Simon of Cyrene to reach Golgotha (Calvary) the place of the skull. Stripped again by soldiers who cast lots for your clothing, you were then laid on the ground and nailed to the cross.

OUR FATHER..., TEN HAIL MARYS..., GLORY BE...

The Crucifixion

Crucified between two thieves, he was raised up from the earth to take on sin and death, to be the sponge that soaks up our sins, to be the drain through which all evil is poured away, for he is our cleansing and our healing. Seeing his anguished mother and Saint John standing near, he said, "Mother, behold your son. Son, behold your mother." And from that moment Saint John took Our Lady into his safe keeping. One of the crucified thieves jeered at him, "If you are the Christ, save yourself and us as well." But the other thief spoke up, "We deserved what we are getting, but this man is innocent. Jesus, remember me when you come into your Kingdom." "I promise you," said Jesus, "this day you will be with me in paradise." He suffered there from the sixth hour to the ninth, while darkness covered the earth, until at last he cried out in a loud voice, "Father, into your hands I commend my spirit," breathed his last and descended into hell, the domain of the dead.

OUR FATHER..., TEN HAIL MARYS..., GLORY BE...

THE GLORIOUS MYSTERIES

THE RESURRECTION

On the third day Jesus was raised from the dead, not brought back to his old life, but taken through death to a new life, leaving his tomb empty. He destroyed death and restored life. He appeared to Mary Magdalene, then to the Apostles a number of times. To prove the reality of his body he invited Thomas to feel his wounds, and he ate fish with the apostles to convince them that he was no ghost, as though saying, "This is really me. This is the body that was nailed to the cross, that was laid in the tomb, but which now is risen." However, he would not let Mary Magdalene touch him, because, he said, he had not yet risen to his Father. He appeared to the apostles in the room where they were without using door or window. And he appeared to the two disciples on the road to Emmaus, but something prevented them from realising who he was until they recognised him in the breaking of bread. His body, was being changed, transformed, transfigured, glorified, a glorification which was completed in his Ascension.

OUR FATHER..., TEN HAIL MARYS..., GLORY BE...

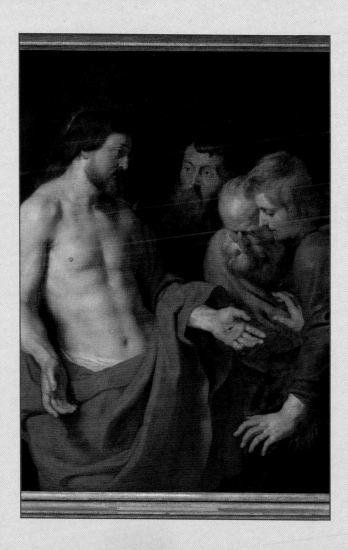

THE ASCENSION

Forty days after the Resurrection, the apostles assembled on the mountain in Galilee as Jesus had directed them. Jesus appeared to them and said, "All authority in heaven and on earth has been given to me. Go, therefore, and make disciples of all nations, baptising them in the name of the Father, and of the Son and of the Holy Spirit, and teach them to observe all that I have commanded you; and, behold, I am with you always, even to the end of the world." As he blessed them, he withdrew from them and was carried up to heaven. The apostles worshipped him, then returned to Jerusalem full of joy. Our human nature, our flesh and bone, our mind and heart, taken on by the Second Person of the Holy Trinity in the Incarnation, purged in his Passion and Death, raised, transformed and glorified in his Resurrection and Ascension, is made fit for heaven, fit to face God for all eternity.

OUR FATHER..., TEN HAIL MARYS..., GLORY BE...

THE DESCENT OF THE HOLY SPIRIT

At Pentecost, fifty days after the Resurrection, the apostles were together in the Upper Room where they were staying, when suddenly there came a sound from heaven like a mighty wind which filled the house. Tongues like fire came and rested on each one of them, and they were filled with the Holy Spirit and began to speak in other languages. The people were astonished because, when the apostles spoke, each person heard them in his or her own tongue. Peter stood up and said, "These men are not drunk. This is what the prophet forecast, that God would pour his Spirit on all flesh, your sons and daughters shall prophesy, your young men shall see visions, and your old men shall dream dreams." The Holy Spirit, the Lord, the giver of life, the very breath of God, dwelt within the apostles, not instead of Jesus, but to make the Risen Jesus present. Jesus had told them of the Holy Spirit as the wind and the fire: the wind that fills our sails, the breeze that calms our fears, the fire that thaws our cold, that warms our hearts, that burns our rubbish, that lights our way. Come, Holy Spirit, fill the hearts of your people and kindle in them the fire of your love.

OUR FATHER..., TEN HAIL MARYS..., GLORY BE...

THE ASSUMPTION OF
OUR LADY INTO HEAVEN

The Orthodox Church teaches that Our Lady died a natural death, was buried, but then was raised in resurrection and was glorified. The Catholic Church teaches that "at the end of her natural life Our Lady was taken body and soul into heaven". It was in her womb and with her consent that the Son of God took on our human nature, was born of her flesh, was nourished by her milk, and, most especially, was loved by her. She gave birth to him and brought him up, and, though a sword of sorrow did pierce her heart, she loved him to the end. No wonder, then, that God should take her home to heaven, her human nature transformed and glorified after the pattern of the Resurrection of her Son and by virtue of it.

OUR FATHER..., TEN HAIL MARYS..., GLORY BE...

The Coronation of Our Lady as Queen of Heaven

Angels cheer and saints rejoice at the entry into heaven and into God's embrace of the Virgin Mother of his Only Begotten Son. God would not allow her to see the corruption of the tomb, but raised her to heavenly heights as a sign of sure hope and comfort for his pilgrim people here on earth. There is no pomp in heaven, but the simple nobility of the handmaid of the Lord is celebrated with great joy and thanksgiving. She glorifies the Lord and rejoices in God her Saviour, for the Almighty has worked marvels for her. The innocent Virgin, the devoted Mother is lifted up and taken home to glorious Resurrection, First Lady of heaven.

OUR FATHER..., TEN HAIL MARYS..., GLORY BE...

THE LUMINOUS MYSTERIES

THE BAPTISM OF THE LORD

At the river Jordan John was preaching a baptism of repentance. He said, "I am the voice of one crying in the wilderness, make straight the way of the Lord. There is one mightier than me who is coming after me. I have baptised you with water, but he will baptise you with the Holy Spirit." Then, when Jesus came to him, John exclaimed, "Behold the lamb of God who takes away the sins of the world !" At the insistence of Jesus, John baptised him in the river Jordan, and a voice came from heaven, "This is my beloved Son in whom I am well pleased." And the Holy Spirit descended on him in the form of a dove. This was the moment chosen by Jesus to launch his public life. His ministry had begun.

OUR FATHER..., TEN HAIL MARYS..., GLORY BE...

THE WEDDING FEAST AT CANA

There was a wedding at Cana in Galilee. Mary was there, and so was Jesus with some of his disciples. During the wedding feast the wine ran out. Mary said to Jesus, "They have no wine." Jesus replied, "What is that to me ? My time has not come yet." His mother said to the servants, "Do whatever he tells you." There were six stone jars standing there, jars which the Jews used in their rites of purification. Each could hold twenty to thirty gallons. Jesus said to the servants, "Fill the jars with water." They filled them to the brim. Then Jesus said to them "Take some out and take it to the steward." They did so, the steward tasted the water which had turned into wine, and exclaimed, "People generally serve the best wine first, but you have kept the best wine until now." This was the first of the signs that Jesus did. His time had come. He changes water into wine, he multiplies loaves and fishes, he walks on water and calms storms. He heals the sick and raises the dead. He is the Lord with the message of eternal life.

OUR FATHER..., TEN HAIL MARYS..., GLORY BE...

THE PROCLAMATION
OF THE KINGDOM

Jesus' proclamation of the Kingdom is always bold and sometimes baffling. Our first step into it is through repentance for our sins, but we have not entered a place, but rather a state. The Kingdom is within us. It is sown like seed and it promises a harvest. It is like yeast leavening a measure of flour. It is like treasure or a perfect pearl, such that we sell everything we have in order to buy it. It is a state of being forgiven, obliging us to forgive those who are in debt to us. It is where justice reigns, but when challenged by Pilate, Jesus said, "My kingdom is not of this world." The Kingdom begins in this world, but it comes to fruition in the next when Jesus Christ, eternal Priest and King of all creation, will make all created things subject to his rule and present to his Father an eternal and universal kingdom, a kingdom of truth and life, a kingdom of holiness and grace, a kingdom of justice, love and peace.

OUR FATHER..., TEN HAIL MARYS..., GLORY BE...

THE TRANSFIGURATION

After Jesus had told the apostles that he must suffer and be put to death, he took Peter, James and John up a high mountain where he was transfigured before their eyes. His face shone like the sun, and his clothes became as white as light. Heaven was shining through him. Moses and Elijah appeared in conversation with him. "It is wonderful for us to be here," said Peter. "I will make three shrines here, one for you, one for Moses and one for Elijah." Suddenly a bright cloud overshadowed them, and a voice came from the cloud, "This is my beloved Son in whom I am well pleased. Listen to him." The three apostles fell on their faces, filled with awe, but Jesus came and touched them. "Stand up," he said. "Do not be afraid." When they opened their eyes they saw only Jesus, who said, "Tell no one about the vision until the Son of Man has risen from the dead." They had been given a foretaste of heaven, a foretaste of what is to happen to the whole of creation at the end of time.

OUR FATHER..., TEN HAIL MARYS..., GLORY BE...

THE INSTITUTION
OF THE EUCHARIST

During his last supper, Jesus took some bread and said, "This is my body". He took some wine and said, "This is my blood", and he distributed both to his apostles. "I am the bread of life," he said. "I am the living bread which has come down from heaven. Anyone who eats this bread will live for ever. For my flesh is real food and my blood is real drink. Whoever eats my flesh and drinks my blood lives in me and I live in them." This is true manna from heaven, the bread of angels, food for pilgrims. At the very beginning God said, "Let there be light, and there was light." God said, let there be sun, moon, land, sea, birds of the air, fish of the sea, man, male and female, in the image and likeness of God Himself. And so it was. God said, and it came to be. Here is the same authority at work in Jesus. Jesus said, "This is my body, this is my blood." This is the executive power of the Word of God. "Take, eat," He said.

OUR FATHER..., TEN HAIL MARYS..., GLORY BE...

IMAGE CREDITS

Image Credits

DC, USA / Bridgeman Images

p39 © Epitaph of Nikolaas Rockox and his wife Adriana Perez, 1513-15 (oil on panel) , Rubens, Peter Paul (1577-1640) / Koninklijk Museum voor Schone Kunsten, Antwerp, Belgium / © Lukas - Art in Flanders VZW / Bridgeman Images

p41 © Vision of St John Evangelist on Patmos, Ascension of Christ among Apostles, or Christ in Glory by Antonio Allegri, known as Correggio (1489-ca 1534), fresco, 966x888 cm diameter at base, detail, Church of St John Evangelist, dome, Parma, 1520-1523 / De Agostini Picture Library / L. Artini / Bridgeman Images

p43 © Pentecost. Miniature of choirbook. 15th-16th century. Archive of Osma-Burgos. Spain. / Archive of Osama Burgos, Castile and Leon, Spain / Tarker / Bridgeman Images

p45 © The Assumption of the Virgin, 1844 (oil on canvas), Janmot, Louis (1814-92) / Musee d'Art Moderne, St. Etienne, France / Bridgeman Images

p47 © The Coronation of the Virgin with Saints Peter, Paul, Ambrose and Charles Borromeo (oil on canvas), Nuvolone, Carlo Francesco (1609-1662) / Private Collection / Photo © Christie's Images / Bridgeman Images

p51 © Baptism of Christ, by Pietro Perugino (ca 1450-1523) / De Agostini Picture Library / G. Nimatallah / Bridgeman Images

p53 © The Marriage Feast at Cana, c.1665-75, Murillo, Bartolome Esteban (1618-82) / The Henry Barber Trust, The Barber Institute of Fine Arts, University of Birmingham / Bridgeman Images

p55 © 'Jerusalem, Jerusalem', illustration for 'The Life of Christ', c.1886-96 (gouache on paperboard), Tissot, James Jacques Joseph (1836-1902) / Brooklyn Museum of Art, New York, USA / Bridgeman Images

p57 © The Transfiguration (oil on canvas), Cesari, Giuseppe (1568-1640) / Ferens Art Gallery, Hull Museums, UK / Bridgeman Images

p59 © The Last Supper, Christ between John and Peter, 1520 ca, Joos van Cleve (1485-1540 ca), altarpiece from the church of Frati Minori in Genoa, Italy, 16th century / Louvre, Paris, France / De Agostini Picture Library / Bridgeman Images

ABOUT THE AUTHOR

Fr Michael Sharkey is a priest of the Archdiocese of Birmingham. A former school teacher, he trained for the priesthood at the Beda College, Rome, and was ordained in 1974. He has worked in a number of parishes, taught at St Mary's Seminary, Oscott, the Gregorian and Angelicum Universities, Rome, worked in the Vatican's Congregation for Catholic Education, represented the Holy See at the Council of Europe on two committees, Education and Sport, and edited the documents of the International Theological Commission, Ignatius Press, 1989, 2009. He is currently parish priest of St Michael's, Sonning Common, South Oxfordshire.

Other Publications by this author:
Stations of the Cross (2018)

NOTES

NOTES

NOTES

NOTES

THE ROSARY
BY
FR MICHAEL SHARKEY

£3.00/€3.75

Publisher to the Holy See
www.alivepublishing.co.uk

9 781906 278274